LIVE IN SUSPENSE

LIVE IN SUSPENSE
by David Groff

TRIO HOUSE PRESS

Copyright © July 1, 2023 David Groff

No part of this book may be used or performed without written consent of the author, if living, except for critical articles or reviews.

Groff, David
1st edition

ISBN: 978-1-949487-15-2
Library of Congress Control Number: 2022949486

Interior design by Hadley Hendrix
Cover art by Michael Brohman
Cover design by Joel W. Coggins
Editing by Kris Bigalk and Natasha Kane

Trio House Press, Inc.
Minneapolis
www.triohousepress.org

again for Clay

Table of Contents

ONE

Live in Suspense	14
Desert Stink Beetle	15
Disbelieving These Deaths, I Go to Sit by Lake Hebron	16
Days of 1980	18
You're in My Light	20
The Changing Table	21
A Boy's Own Jesus	22
Chaff	23
My Mother	25
Suspense	27
Photobomb, Taos	28
Days of 1985	29
You Kids Get Off My Lawn	32
I with No Rights in This Matter	33
Dead Deer	34

TWO

Glass House	38
Prodigal	40
I'm Here to Help:	43
Hit the Road, Jack	44
A Boy's Own Bible Story	45
What Else	47
Malcah	48
His Corpse	49
A Boy's Own Bible Story	50
Write About Somebody's Else's Family!	52
Call Your Father	54
Little Invocation	55

A Boy's Own Bible Story	56
Revival	57
All the Nights	58
420, A.M.	59
Grievance	60

THREE

Days of 1986	64
Gribbles	65
Days of 1992	66
Infinitive	68
Birthday Wish	70
An Avocado for My Mother	71
A Boy's Own Heaven	72
His Craft	74
Days of 1996	75
After a Time I Touch My Husband	76
Turn	77
Where Is the Lady	79
Like a Simile	81
I Want to Be Alone	83
Snow Melting	84
Nights of 2027	85
Suspense	87
A Friend Asks Me to Pray for the Soul of His Dead Brother	88
The World Without Me	89

Notes	93
Acknowledgments	95
About the Author	97
About the Artist	99

Suspense—is Hostiler than Death—
Death—tho'soever Broad,
Is Just Death, and cannot increase—
Suspense—does not conclude—

But perishes—to live anew—
But just anew to die—
Annihilation—plated fresh
With Immortality—
             — Emily Dickinson

This suspense is terrible. I hope it will last.
      — Oscar Wilde

ONE

Live in Suspense

I leave Clay
but just for a weekend. Business.
Los Angeles, so the risk is minimal.
Still. Each parting is practice.
It's a little death, what Donne
and the others called orgasm,
that intense suspension
a squeezing out the Metaphysicals
said we didn't remake,
not a river but a draining lake.
I embrace this shrug of separation,
the unbrushed goodbye at 6 AM,
the plunge in the stomach as the elevator
plunges downward, as the plane
will not plunge, probably,
nor will the Lyft crash on La Cienega
or the boulevard fall into fissures;
nor will Clay's bike collide
with a truck on Route 9,
plunging him down a Palisade.
Every risk is a rehearsal.
We know what chance does.
We know what death does,
will do, has to do.
Our bridges still hold us
though their cables quiver.
Which is why when I kiss Clay
I recall how HIV, unchecked,
made our every day a next-to-last,
urgent as orgasm, until
it was tamed as truth and metaphor.
Which is why when I kiss Clay
I taste the dust of his tongue.
Re-erected with desire,
we are meta-physical,
the little death a resonance away.
Leaving him, I return to him.

Desert Stink Beetle

You who gave your wings for more water,
evolving to adhere them to your thorax
until you became a shiny black capsule,
a desert death-reaper, a hearse of a bug,

nosing the dirt as if you hunt your glasses,
your butt in the sky like a hi-rider,
comically somber, somberly comic,
your exhaust your line of defense,
the twenty-inch ray of spray
you emit to get the last word,
a stink you survive that lets you survive,

     —my darkling,

my thick drop of unmooned night,

let me persist as your species,
submit my wings to my torso,
commit myself to ground,
make my diet detritus and shit,

evolve to be unlovely,
a black ruby of gloom,
a fecal American scarab,

behind my earth-ridden face
my breath all bad,
my ass in the air my moon,
ready to let it out,
ready to take it in.

Disbelieving These Deaths, I Go to Sit by Lake Hebron

A thunderstorm has spun from a near-blue sky,
then faded like a tantrum, the child sunny and unharmed.
Warmth like a human's breath shrugs off the fall wind.
The lake is only mildly disturbed; it didn't know
the deceased, so its sympathies don't extend to empathy
and it's a lake, not a pathetic fallacy, though I try.
I work to stay here, not to be netted
to various keenings. Hard to do even on a good day.
In the shallows are the slabs of slate
like coffins fallen off a truck, each one
not containing a body I knew, although slate caskets
irretrievable in water speak to me. They inform me
that if I were really here I'd notice the cloud
very like a whale until it blossoms like a poppy, fast.
A chorus of dead from a chorus of caskets
ought to open their lids and shoulder out their slabs
to walk on water.
My dead father would eye the lake for plops of fish
he could catch and feel guilty for eating, eye to eye,
though he was dubious of lakes, preferring currents,
local water strung to seas, which lets me see him
as a river, bodies of water as bodies,
as metaphors, including the Babylon waters of weeping.
My mother, city born, should
stride to me across the tidelessness,
the wind revealing her girlish nape,
and George my most recent dead guy, cleared
of the thunder behind his brow and now,
rise right here, part of the democracy of day,
along with Daniel Crisman, 25, dead on 9/11,
eighteen years ago today, a man I know from a poster
gladly diving at 43 into this crisp water,
warmer than dying young. All my loves
with AIDS, the guys who I drag everywhere,
Ron, Len, Craig, Jay, Paul, Mark, John,
Tom, Richard, the armada ghosting the cove,
their wakes cut short, should land on the island I am.
Hebron, the first city, arid, blazes from across the ocean
its millennia of murders, histories bleeding into each other,

torches and missiles and rifles like lake lightning.
Children killed in cars or cages—they should splash.
All of these once knew the word for *lake*,
said *lake*, swam in a lake of genuine water,
fell through the frosty metaphor of lake,
their lips too blue and sewn ever to say *lake* again.
Here they are none of them at all,
evaporated out of time until I become
a lake nobody swims in. Again the trees tremble,
the clouds lower their cliché of brow,
the water snaps like a shroud.
It is a day in September, more thunder to come.
The lake is alive with togue, perch, and bass.

Days of 1980
    for Mike Messenger

I keep coming back to his back,
the first expanse of skin
I was close enough to kiss,
skin I thought I memorized
like a map in the light of night,
I a boy let out
beyond my body's fence
to play in the field of a man,
having blown him badly,
unattuned to cock
but loving its pink delight,
tender and hard at once,
as it spasmed, then recoiled,
when he rolled over himself
to present his prairie of lats,
a gift and a reprimand
in the absence of his face
as he pretended to sleep,
my brash breath on his spine
as I charted his specks and moles,
the sunspots I didn't know
could kill him years from now,
I the gangly boy
Jesus-haunted but hungry,
now rife with eerie relief,

Mike knowing what I could not,
that I was too new to be good,
too full of sudden need
for him to be able to bear,
wounded as he was
by arrows I almost saw,
wizened at twenty-nine,
arsoned by his life,
("he has no crust," said his dad,
later, when Mike fled),

and so we lay awake,
spoons differently magnetized,
the tiny gap in our years
in 1980
as large as the Middle Ages
meeting the Renaissance,
he the striated saint
burned umber in his desert,
I the reckless explorer
plunging like sun into fog,

and all of this just before AIDS
and its fucking metaphors,
the symbolism of beds
we made and had to lie in,
the beds we had to die in,
the lovers turned for good,

as I come back to his back,
in Iowa City, Iowa,
two men in a single bed
speaking lung to lung,
mediated by ribs,
waiting for the sun
to end the ruse of sleep,
who kiss with eyes half-shut.

You're in My Light

said my father to his boy
when I leaned under his lamp,
crawling against his wingback
in my short joy.

I never got that he meant
I darkened his text,
could never connect
my shadow, his head bent.

I thought I cast no shade,
that my body was just myself,
apprentice to his mass.
But I had the shape to have made

myself a power of dark.
I thought I could see to read
in any light God shed,
sunlight or spark.

Now he is dead, past text,
no light at all in his lap.
You're in my light
and I can't see what's next,

he says. I say back,
You're in my light.
And so we share our shade,
both of us light and its lack.

The Changing Table

The wallpaper, blue with pink and white mums
afloat above me, a baby's sky, and I
lying spread below, feet in the air,
the air, the table, the parts of me
one with my mother's hands,

and I feel in my brain a tiny growth,
some new nerve blooming
into a knowing that I know
not her body but this body,
a learning of my lines,

    as those two mother hands,
    those probably necessary hands,
    the probably innocent hands
    like bees commandeer me—
    cheeks, penis, legs, brain—

        and here I am wafting to the wallpaper
        in a swarm of smoke, a little sacrifice,
        to lose myself in the sky of flowers,
        my body down there a split seed pod.
        I fly up here my entire life.

A Boy's Own Jesus

The older brother I never had,
the one who knew the way
to the bathroom in the dark.
Okay with rushed prayers.
He who witnessed the fists
gut me to breathlessness.
Able to sleep during storms.
Trustworthy, though with
erratic tempests,
like a father after a few drinks.
Never a father.
Keeping distance
from his own hard father.
Suffering little children
who suffered, yet suffering
when I lay my weight on him
and made his thighs tingle.
Shaking his head at my penis
pronging, this pollution,
this boy-distraction.
Looking good in a loincloth,
his pained muscles
turning me truant.
Desire and dying,
made one body.
In my fevers
rising with robe-wings
over my wild boat,
feeling fevered too,
keen to each degree.
Making me his special boy.
His arms held and wrestled me.
A cradle or a cage,
devil or deliverer.

Chaff

On this scorching seventh day at 10
God harvests the town and scatters
us unbelievers to our Sunday funk:

my heart rate monitor ticking my pace,
I am the blackbird seeking glean,
Magdalene the streetwalker.

In her own parched plot Mary,
all white, crisp as a blank check,
spreads for me her wings of sleeve,

sharp as a pillar of salt, eyes cast
down as if I bring unbearable heat.
She seems machine-forged, a cast

of thousands, lips dead-nurse pale,
hardly a sister to the possibly real
Mary the mystified mother,

feeding chickens in her son's sawdust,
fretted by questions and flies.
Hello, fake momma, St. Facsimila.

I pant to the Methodist jumble of brick,
its stained glass dark with daylight,
sealed as tight as Rubbermaid,

whose congregants, says Reverend Dad,
all proper shopkeepers, have eyes set
too close together; but I lack

the method to test his prejudice
against the selection of Presbyterians—
the lesser gentry (he believes)—

I gasp past disembarking their Buicks,
assured that God is Rotarian emeritus,
their sanctuary brutal as a school,

on its forthright façade a Jesus wrought
in white steel like an Xmas reindeer,
its arms a scarecrow of welcome.

The choir, heads bleached to wheat,
fans itself with bulletins, ascends its steps,
eyes me, dis-elects my sweat.

I home of sorts to St. Monica's,
patron saint of errant children,
Episcopal, gothic but cramped,

the dowager's heirloom watch.
From inside wafts the faintest organ
and I inhale childhood: wine and wax,

the must of God's interior, the paschal
candle guttering in the rim of summer.
It pierces me like the centurion's spear.

I am closer to death than I am
to the acolyte picking the carpet
clean of his father's crumbs

and being so deadly requires
I bind my heart with this strap
and mind and measure my step

to pump my number as long as I can,
because I have a finite set of Sundays
and I am burning.

My Mother

Still she is an other.
My fears make her
remote as a last ridge

rife with veins and caves
(the conceits of veins and caves),
slippery, scary to climb,

her summit crowned in cloud.

Witnessed from death's distance,
her lovely skirt swaying,
she carries along her frame,

but I lose her in my mystery.

Still she blooms somewhat,
as if stepping forward from her body
into the character I love

with all my failings.
I try not to falter further,

not to deny in her
her half-fathomed humanness
and make of her another relation—
mother, producer, a kind of partner—

I a male full of males,
of female born.

Mother, you of unswum pools,
your grotto so deep
I shy in the shallows,

I reach across to offer
you my myopic eye,

I lose my footing,
I breaststroke to you,

you a woman full of yourself,

swimming to an inseparation
until with your lost body
you might give me birth again.

SUSPENSE

At last I have learned to shut up.
You squint, pause, shiver,
seized by silence,
in New York a negative soliloquy.

I've grown into the sense
not to tender chatter,
not to let panic preside,
to reside inside myself,

and let our absence be presence.
Still, your eclipse of sound
darkens our table. I know
once you speak, we change.

What secret will you share?
By not asking, do I betray you?
Will love or death, large or small,
rise like a sun or a beast?

This restaurant is wrestling voices.
This espresso is getting cold.
I listen to your eyes.
I live in suspense.

Photobomb, Taos

The sky on the butt side of sunset is
a veiny blue, the clouds vapor-trailish
but not jet-made, probably, below
a mountain that looks like a mountain.

I don't know its first name or its tales.
Its greens go gray with drought & dusk
but still it's strewn with glare,
hard to look at, a lung-busting climb.

Trees like brandy snifters dot the plain:
vases in a cemetery with flat plaques.
Did they know to grow here, or
who punched in seeds to snare the dirt?

Ebbing from them to me is grass,
darkening, like a wave of dishwater,
like a baby's hair as she grows up,
but some clumps gather, dirty gold,

baskets for me to fill or burn.
After them, at the toes of my Keds,
a shadow interrupts us from the west.
Shadow: the sun's dead end.

It echoes the mass of mountain,
messing up the postcardy view
like a starved coyote or a sundial.
I know that shadow's name.

Days of 1985
  St. Vincent's Hospital, Greenwich Village, & Environs

We lay out hope on the tray,
its puréed entree
slid under the door.
We hold out hope
but our arms
stress at the joints
& ulna bone.
Masters make their slaves
in games of sex and power
hold this position
but they hold
it out of adoration.
Also our knees hurt, which,
if we fell to pray
would, like hell, burn.
Hope takes time,
takes it hour by hour,
turns time into a tiny step:
his totter to the five and dime,
his tears on the stoop,
his vomit by the mailbox.
Hope's in the palm of our hand today,
not in a shy, sly hand once holding
hands across the handkerchief display.
Hope takes the cake and day.
Two adages: hope's an early worm,
any drowning port inside the storm.
Call hope obligation.
Call it clouded sun
& silvered cloud,
or sub & dom,
lash & tongue.
Call it on the phone,
rotary dial, the dial
tone ungodly loud.
Believe it's in the bone,
avow it might abide,
squirm at yeah or nope,

hope a rope
to hang hope on.
A small-business holding.
Hope is day by goddamn day.
It is tide,
it tides us over,
a half a teaspoon
swallowed, none
of it held down,
or if held down
half bile.
Hope: an unscrewed railing.
A magazine's thinnest issue.
It goes south.
It's a bracelet lacking charms.
Hope is nearly our
ruination,
Solomon's little foxes
gnawing on our vine.
Hope never is in clover.
Hope—get out of your rut!
No. Hope says *soon*.
Does it trump his disposition,
his Adam's apple
not too visible,
the skull-seeing stare
pulsing with tissue-
paper prayer?
No. It's ifs, ands, & buts. But
still, say a prayer for José, Stuart,
Tynell, Iris. The many Daves.
Hope is such a bitch.
Hope sits in a mouth;
its kiss may be a germ.
(We don't push the point.)
Hope is the final floor.
Hope is risible
for Josh or Steven.
For Roy Cohn, even.
Hope is a failing,
routine nation.

It is an enfolding
infolding like an ear,
hearing being the last to go.
Hope is a possibly magic ray gun.
Hope is no Ronald Reagan.
Hope goes fast and slow.
Hope hopes against hope.
Not all hope is gone
except for Steven.
("There's no hope!"
cried Ron.
Ron is gone.)
Hope is out of love.
It is right here,
it is over there.
it holds its breath in air
we breathe in,
in hope
of
exhalation.

You Kids Get Off My Lawn

I've never tasted the cum
of a man who wasn't me.
Imagine that if you can,
you 21st century men:
I can't remember a heat
direct on my dick against
a lover's inner membrane.
My men and my times required
a rubber and dis-ease.
No matter your miracle,
for me every fuck is a threeway
with you know who.

And here you're all released,
early out of school,
none of you doomed to repeat
the history you forget,
living skin to skin,
the virus expensively tamed
and sex a possible game,
its tricks and traumas routine,
not your father's Oldsmobile.

You kick up your heels in my sprinkler,
dousing yourself to the bone,
your laughter not sympathetic
but not derisive either.

I won't turn off my hose.
I watch from the porch with my ghosts.
If you look hard into my shade
you'll see me in you.

I with No Rights in This Matter

All day I have been looking for my children
who I know will never exist.
I do not find them in the forms of my students
though I would pluck them out of traffic
as if my genes were speaking. Nor are my children
my nieces and nephews whose blood bears
resemblances to my own, in whom I echo.
They have parents to belong to, and I borrow them.

Tangled amid the toddlers in strollers,
the elementary kids skipping beside their dads to school,
the ten-year-olds walking boldly alone
past the chanting man and the compost bin,
the sullen or screeching teens all angry angles,
their parents practiced men and women
who once as babies might have sat on my lap
and now run enterprises,
                         I am where among them?
My non-procreation seemed the condition of my freedom,
I who swept from man to man, who lived like a boy,
who felt like no one's father, not even his own,
who in the prime of his sperm suspected his semen was deadly,
who saw men of a generation give birth to death,
his ejaculations dead ends, ciphers of surges and love,
who can't run fast enough to catch the fading train.

Still I feel in the fork of my jeans
those millions I produce even now,
however warped and bent, clamoring
to make half the child I will not make,
striving inside me as I try to bear
the mostly straight world's stranger-children,
offspring owned by no one, really,
amazing in their incipient decay,
stray as leaves and already scattering,
running to the risk of the intersection,
all of them my letters to God on the street.
I let them go ahead of me.

Dead Deer

Bolt, thwarted vault, late brake,
gasp of impact, temblor of thud—
the beast drops on the blade of hood,
ribs rip from their roots, hearts seize,
the windshield goes dark as an eyelid
curtaining to a horizon of blood,
black glass laced with lightning—

I am hit with wheel, steel, doe
embracing me backward as speed
crushes me forward into
a bursting hug, sternums to spines,

past last words,
no extra second to
follow the plan to tell
God I am sorry, no foxhole repentance,
no appeal to the fate-maker,
my sentence incomplete, a
fragment, a run-on,

no scenes spun out so fast
that the brain convulses with
conclusion and love—

I do not even think of you,
give no torn word for
you to live by—

I mesh corpse into carcass,
I am dead, dear,
I leave you my velocity
and there at the edge of the road
I give you my fawn.

TWO

Glass House

In the pantry looking for rice
I hear a punch against the wall
and imagine an outlet poofing,
the power I depend on gone.
But no, at the entrance on the slate
outside a bird is on its back, in a spasm –
it hit the great window of the house I stay in.
It flutters as if in anger, to right itself,
as if like an athlete it would shake off,
unclench itself to clench again,
and then it stops as if lost in shock
that the rules for flying changed without a word,
that it isn't gliding into that shiny sky.

Useless, I wait. I hope the bird won't bleed,
red seeping into its smoke-taupe feathers,
that it will still collect itself, flip over, fly.
But that was a violent strike on the glass.
I wish I knew its name. I know birds
die all the time, from falcons, hawks,
cats, quick snakes, a lightning strike,
my fellow humans looking for a meal.
Last night my dinner was a bird.
But a single bird against a window,
witnessed, feels like tragedy, or pity.
I do my vigil, I get the rice, I monitor.
No movement. I listen for other frantic,
angry, grieving birds. No luck.
Do birds like elephants lament their kind
or does the wind push birds along?

At last I get the broom, the dust pan,
flip it in—so light, of course,
such tensile, aerodynamic bones,
a human hand, a grayed glass chalice—
and take it to the creek grass, hoping
for a turkey vulture, a bird for a bird,
that hungry, useful cannibal mortician.
I say words of consolation and complicity.

I use my hand as if to bless or wave.
The world needs stickers on its windows.
I go back to the mirror of my house.
She was, I learn, a mourning dove.

Prodigal

When we moved our father out
of his stuffed and stuffy house
to the dark brightness of LA
and the attention of my brother,

his place lay furnished but vacant,
a memory, a hope, and a lie.
Someday, he said, he'd be spry
enough to climb on the train

in downtown LA, span
the curve of the country, and come
back to his wrinkled Cape Cod
and its somnolent eyebrow dormers.

"It's an Addison museum!"
I told him when he ventured,
and he ventured often, to ask
us keepers of his flame

about the one home he'd owned.
As with the churches he'd tended,
he wanted it to miss him,
to be staggered by lament

but also to prosper because
he was the man who made it
a place that could not live
without his ministrations.

The house, no childhood home,
held grief like a grudge,
stuck in the soybean fields,
all evenings descending blue,

the fluorescence of Bob Evans
a dinner's respite. My mother
grew bored to her death in that box,
her editing gigs and her sons

arriving less than they left.
Early one Valentine's Day
she grabbed once at her chest
and died in the dining room.

You see why I hated revisits,
you see why I shunned
the four hour schlep from the city
to this landing strip of a state,

you understand why it was I
who never opened the house
to the scouring outside breezes,
never blasted the heat to

burn out all of its wet,
never lingered to notice
the green creep up the walls
and never admitted the smell

that gave the place the sweet
organic aroma of death.
It was as if my father's house
had mortgaged me to the teeth

and I, absent heir of the lord,
drunk with my own regret,
let the Vandals have
the run of my father's fief.

My father's spine-split books,
the cameras' cracked accordions,
the sheepskin of diplomas,
the piano's rusty intestines,

the paintings he painted so badly,
the clothes his mother sewed,
the suits his father preached in,
stereopticon slides of France,

snapshots bleeding to glue,
the *Child's Garden of Verses*
I'd read in my sickly bed,
the vestments my father kept,

the journals I stained as a teen,
the yearbooks in which my mother
grinned like a careless girl,
every porous thing—

I handed it over to mold,
to a green that parodied spring,
to a prison of decomposure,
to a stink that won't come clean.

All was pulled out and tossed,
the clocks and dishes sold.
My brother, a hero, labored
with me to scrape out the ship.

In my father's LA flat
there is no mold, just dust.
Most of what he'd held
for the time that Jesus would call

him and his trucks of stuff
is lost to the curse of must.
He will bear no gifts for his maker.
I go naked before the Lord.

I'm Here to Help:

your dramaturge, your best investor,
Watson, Joseph Severn, Nelly Dean,
Horatio with your flight of angels,

the buddy waving your muddy flag
on Posterity Street, near Oblivion Place,

an executor who polishes your urn,
contracted in some silky pact
to handle your extended run,

I the guy who shirks the glare,
ensuring any light that picks me out

shrugs off to you and buffs you up—
and not just you but all of you,
you entire cast of unshot stars,

I the one who rolls away the stone
for every one of you who glowed and died,

a man's best friend, the last man standing,
the one escaped to tell
the not-yet-wasting news of you,

surviving so we all survive for now,
our sentence incomplete.

Hit the Road, Jack
Cedars-Sinai Medical Center, 1/20/18

Impatient, raging at his refusing mouth,
I escape to the Ray Charles Cafeteria
which is not the Ray Charles of cafeterias.
I still see the urine bag, too little filled.
In just an hour my brother will relieve me,
spend the night on a cot, and I'll escape
into Los Angeles, its upright bodies,
its abandoned glare and shiny dark.
What a bad, atonal son I am,
my father my sick warden. When I inch
to the elevator, rise, and stray to his door,
I find him in the lime-green dark
pulling at blanket, shrugging out of bed,
tethered to the tubes that could tear him.
Drugged into sleep that wasn't sleep,
he wants to lead me down Route 66,
reverse the pioneer route, to the Lincoln Highway,
back to his frontier, the Lancaster County corn.
I could sing a hymn. Turn on the light.
I say to him, Just breathe. My brother arrives
and like a deadbeat dad I kiss my father and flee,
say I'll see him in the morning.
                                            But I can't.
When dawn hits the streets we're each free to go.

A Boy's Own Bible Story

The weatherman is really mad.
Bad day, bad year. No one appreciates
him. All the effort he makes to make
sun come up, moon go down,
rain to green up things, wind to blow seeds,

and still his beneficiaries do their business
without sufficient thank-you notes,
preferring their fetishes and conveniences,
the distractions of bickering and killing.

The weatherman is profoundly offended.
Such ingrates! One lonely day,
his headache a thunderstorm,
he decides to declare rain for almost a month and a half.
He sticks his hand outside the window
and rain slaps his palm like a coin—
hot rain, skin-scalding rain.

Bodies float up from the earth, fathers clutch children,
mothers try to tie them to tall chimneys and buoyant doors,
single people hold shoulders and kick,
the old sinking first, their white hair a starburst,

but it would take a miracle to float for six weeks,
so every being that takes breath with their nostrils,
including horses, puppies, and salamanders,
inhales water and dies desperate, confused.

No more ingratitude from them!
The weatherman feels his tension headache fade
and a certain release at the base of his spine.

—One man who had sent copious thank-you notes
got a heads-up from the weatherman
who provided precise scientific instructions
on how to build a boat and corral replacement stock:

you can imagine the smell in those stalls
and staterooms after weeks of rain and bloating
and the family dinners of meat and grievance.
You can imagine how grateful they are
to see the weatherman's land.

The weatherman finally has a boatload of love.
See his smile? It's a rainbow of locusts.

What Else

What else can you demand of me?
Bloody knees on the anniversary
of the day you died unseen in your sleep?
When your father gave up the ghost you gave up
the piano for life, and after a year
you ached to play again and guiltily did.
I gave up nothing, my year a grievous ease.
Should I bring the bishop back to your plot
to say a few more last loving words that you,
bashful, a man demandingly underloved,
sought again and again like a dad's caress?
No, better I dig you up and put you
back in your throne of recliner—
I'd do that if I really loved you, you say
or almost say. I'd reignite you,
flick on CNN, bring in grandkids
with their posies and flattering questions,
get you on Facebook with a thousand likes—
I'd do what God it seems cannot
or will not do in the Lancaster winter
of your dead cemetery. That's what I'd do
if I were as good a son as Jesus Fucking Christ
and creation spun on the axis of Addison,
I a Mary Magdalene crowbarring the tomb.

Malcah
    —*noun,* queen. *Hebrew.*

The mother, deprived, needed more than could be provided;
I strained to serve as her first son.

She sang songs from WWI with her father that she sang
again, but who would listen? Not I, clearly her worst son.

Growing old, she grew bereft of earlier selves
and caressed my hand hard. A coerced son,

I put my hand away and kept courteous distance
but still there lay in me a thirst, a sun-

parched need to crawl against who she was,
the urgent, regnant mother, to be a nursed son.

Dead, she lay like a patient awaiting resuscitation
and I stood stupid beside her, the failed surgeon.

What tribute now can I tender
to restore what I did not give her—what reversion?

—*None,* she comes to say, *I am past your laudation,
my Beloved; you are in me always, my averse son, my immersed son, my
    cursed son.*

His Corpse

This body once included a throat
used to exhale a final thousand words,
help me help me help me help me help me

in its final week, addressing sons or God,
and look at it now, scooped out,
embrined, sealed shut, no way

to sound out its fiddler crab of shell,
to press my ear against its heart
then rip its lips apart and strip its glue,

drain its fluids for my mouth-to-mouth,
and force my breath in and out
to stun it out of posthumousness,

(the hair parted wrong, he'd hate that,
the mouth a seam of disdain,
the hands—why were they hidden?),

to inflate its echoes, to stun into life,
to pluck it from its oblong furniture,
to snatch it like a ruby off its satin,

to redo its sentence and infinitives,
the carcass good for nothing but
this expensive remembrance

exempt from its own heartache,
never inclining its ear to hear my
help me help me help me help me help me

A Boy's Own Bible Story

The father had business with his son.
They went mountain climbing,
taking firewood with them—
curious, but maybe trees didn't grow
at the height they were going.
The father had his boss on his mind,
heard his boss's words in his head,
and a boss is a boss.

He told the son to carry the wood.
The son asked what they would grill.
The dad said God would provide.

The father built the fire,
then he jumped his son,
wrestled him down expertly
and tied him up.

                    Imagine the son
freaked and screaming,
twisting, un-understanding
                    as you might not understand.
His sound went up the mountain, up to
the sunny sky.

The father took out
his Swiss Army knife,
the longest blade, and raised it.
He felt bad but a job is a job.
Pleading and screams. Just screams.

Then the boss called—
mission aborted.
You got with the program,
said the dad's head.

Dad said the son didn't struggle, gave in,
that the convenient sheep,
horns stuck, surrendered.

Imagine that son.
Chronicle that cannibal feast.

Write About Somebody Else's Family!

cried my father when he saw
there on the dining room table
my college notebook open,
expecting a Grecian urn and finding
Uncle Grant's hand on my leg—

the dining room spinning, flung up,
a tilt-a-whirl, the lace
of the table sliding,
my feet scrabbling—

I was so wrong to
do this, to write it,
my face felt scraped
all the way down to
my felt thigh,
left thigh, gripped
again and again,
up and around,
by Uncle Grant's hand,
testing my muscle—

Uncle Grant, dead ringer
for the grim farmer
of American Gothic,
driving up my bloodstream
in the forest-green
Buick Electra he replaced
every second year,
the car whose armrest
I half-sat on,
scooching to elude
Uncle Grant's right hand
on the way to the fishing hole,

he the wise guide to bait,
eyes mostly lying
on the road, mostly.
Bad faith on a stick.

If only the Buick's door
had snapped open like
a crocodile's kindly jaw
and hurled me on the highway,
roadburn like roadkill,
but the locks were automatic
and this boy was polite.

Now I was the whispering one,
the insinuation,
eating paper

in a boy's own prison
where the family of hiding
hides the strayed son
and strips him of
his penis and pen until now.

Call Your Father

Every night I called you,
    dutiful but game—
my distraction palled you,
    talk a flat flame.

But still we made a noise,
    old father, aging son,
a waltz between us boys,
    14 minutes, done.

A shrink I know says males
    relate best shoulder to shoulder.
Otherwise contact pales
    and they get colder.

But we had nothing to do,
    no tools to make an object.
It was just we two,
    ourselves our subject.

Still, one day proposed a next,
    the day's complaints a refrain,
a litany, a semi-sacred text:
    an ankle ache, a shooting pain.

Now when I call your phone
    I get a recorded answer.
No person picks up, I'm alone,
    I'm a single dancer.

Little Invocation

Dead mother, come lie with me,
hold your old son
as you did in my boy-fever,
snatching me back delirious
as the avalanche smashed
my one flower.
                   Here
in this bed of my age
present your sage self
who in life chose a child
to love beyond price.
Beside me, rise, rest.
Let me sense the heft of your breasts,
the place of your thighs
I sprang from—
                   spread
the wing of your hand
on my eyes so I sleep.

A Boy's Own Bible Story

You can make me clean,
say I the leper to the teacher.
He touches my patches as no man
has touched me since
I was a boy as smooth as dirt.

Like a miracle, my stigmata
unstains. *Tzaraath* vanishes.
I fall, a human thank-you, but
No, go tell just the priest,
not the swarm who ahh.

Yes, I say. Still, I can't
shut my reimagined
mouth. It unseals
a hymn of love so strong
it sics the sick on him.

But who can trust
a boy uncrusted as I am,
his guilt gone to grace,
touched in the head,
his purity curious?

No one will have me,
cleansed because I asked,
earth's exception,
forbidden fruit.
I grow away from touch:

I wander like Lazarus,
alive and too well.
The teacher I love goes on
and I live in my desert
unmarked for forty years.

REVIVAL
    for Ron Haefka

We made a list of every state
we each had sex in. You won
with 31, delighted: summer stock.
Though fifty now and dead, you reappear
made up and young at Community Stage
in Quarryville in a weekend's perfs
of *You Can't Take It with You*:
the suitor, sneaky, keen for fireworks,

puppyish, blond again, the shot at sex
an encore in eyes I almost know.
On the barn of stage a shooting star,
you strut like a Saturday out of town—
my applause enfolds you like the shroud
Ophelia wore, or Mercutio.

All the Nights

when I washed no dishes and left them to her,
her every entreaty ignored and nearly unheard.
The T-shirts peeled off inside-out for her wash,
the trash uncollected in favor of television.
All the breakfasts rushed, lunches bagged, sons roused.

How tired she was of tasks, how weary of harrying.
I spun like the young in the sphere of myself,
a mother a tool, an attendant, a nuisance, a given.

All the slogging occasions undated, unthanked.
Now she has died and cannot be thanked.

Tonight all the nights rise in one dailiness,
the son I didn't have his own resentful presence:

I wash the glass and dry it and put it back,
peel off my shirt so it is not inside out,
breathe the trash with its overripe fruit
and tell my mother I'll take it out in the morning.

420, A.M.

Into our window creeps a burning skunk
from a story below. I don't wake up to debunk
the marijuana minute of drifting up and out,
or the solitary body faith that comes about
when THC dopamines the dawn, and nausea
vaporizes into appetite—let us pause a

moment to appreciate the need a few
have for the specific one or two
burnt offerings cannabis provides:
hunger amid cancer and, for most, the slide
into a being contained in our self, to thrive
as one person sated for a bit. I felt that in 1995.
We make the time we need to play alone.

So, downstairs in the dark a guy gets stoned
as Monday dawns around him, on-demand,
while a flight above we stir and stand,
aching into the day, two middle-aged lovers,
stale-breathed, in stupor with each other,
no longer spinning out our single druthers,

each waking up unfree of the other,
each man made from the men we are, our skunk
the sweat we made asleep. Our spunk.
Grieved and aggrieved, with contact highs,
we kiss good morning, and we rise.

Grievance

Where did you go, grief?
Seems like you want to run away from home.
Don't you know my mother is still dead?
Didn't you hear my father summon you
and bequeath you in his will to me?
Don't you know the names of my spent men?
Won't you still bury your face in your fists
when the dog's choke chain punctures her,
the girl eats clay for lunch,
or children's bodies blow to shore?
You are derelict today,
bingeing on beliefs and newborn babes,
a sunny turn of weather or of praise.
Where did you put my beleaguerers?
What did you do with my asbestos clock?
Where's your leaden shawl?
Here I am as if exempt from you,
my private belly full, my cells secure,
my lover still alive one room away.
Come home to me, grief,
in your garish, happy costume—
don't leave me to savor the rest of my days.

THREE

Days of 1986

My suspect blood.
Dr. Siroty filled a vial
I had to take myself
down the grim avenue
to the Board of Health
in the cold spring evening,
crosswalk after crosswalk
as the sun sidled in.
I saw hundreds of others
like me bearing their blood
but inside their bodies.

The vial—I wanted to pluck it
from my backpack and
prop it on top of a pay phone
or stash it in the trashcan
with the dead Daily News,
wanting no news, not even
good news, all news cleaving
me from my brothers.

But I kept taking steps,
the street annoying with life,
the sun incumbent,
the storefronts bloody gold,
until I had to enter
the Board of Health to find
an unguarded tray of vials
and place mine among them,
all of us numbered,
together in our before.

I went back into a city
vital with night,
the world a blade
so cutting that at times
I could feel I could feel.

GRIBBLES

What you do to driftwood,
eating the strayed freight of trees,
doing what salt does
or the tides' task,
you do to my boat:
shipworms, termites of the sea,
isopods gnawing at the hull,
one twenty-fifth of an inch
of mouth and execution,
grateful as worms can be
to swell your multitudes,

advancing your cause within
barges, pilings, and boats,
passport and transport.
I enable your damage,
my travel my craft's undoing.
I raise my boat to dry dock
and scrape it of you, beings
I can't look in the eye as you rise
from the water and die,
you minute raindrops of sun,
my passengers, my plagues.

Even if I make you a decoy
of beam along my keel,
give you your tariff,
the *wormshoe* you eat,
you still skirt its creosote
and open your jaws wider
to your hunger the longer
I stay away from shore:
go forth and multiply,
you golden cancers of my plans,
break me open and down.

DAYS OF 1992
    Fire Island Pines, some July night

I sat in a crowded hot tub
naked with William Smith,
a journalist, I think,
his chest hair wet and straight,
his head combed with care
even in the steam.
Our eyes met somewhat.
Deep in the water's churn
I put my toe
against his butt hole
and he put his toe
against my butt hole—
I alongside Cavafy
recall the ins and outs
after thirty years.

Toweled off, in a bed,
discussing fucking,
he wanted not to hear
my question on HIV.
In our discordant honesty,
my shrinking fear,
his bruised eyes,
and our safe try,
we ebbed.

Later as he edged
closer to dying,
he gave me a heart,
the size of sand dollar,
metallic, purplish, weighty,
in a purple velvet pouch.
An invitation, talisman,
dismissal, reprimand:
he didn't say, I didn't ask.
I said just thank you.

His name is too common to Google,
that tool and term and world
he wouldn't know.
Whatever place he came from
lies as lost as Alexandria.

I truly do feel
his toe and mine,
our risky holes,
the tide of steam,
as we rose and hugged and
rubbed our chests together,
our blood thudding in the heat.
He was one of the quicker men to go,
before Clinton felt our pain.

Now I'm holding his purple heart.
It's heavy to heft or clasp.
William, I have questions to ask.

INFINITIVE
    to Clay

To yelp for no food, to
beg just a little, then to loll

to get noticed by
a master who, to get you

to roll over, flicks two
fingers—too much to

think about too long, the
verb-thing of uninflected

unattachment, taken
out of agency, away

from object, not at one
with the sentence with

its sententious intention
yet in an infinite syntax,

all sideways figure eights,
a sort of square root,

but still subject to being
a subject or simply

a modifier.
To live,

to be unbound
by living, is to

sate a hunger
to hunger,

to say *stay*,
to act as your own act

to lessen deficit
but be satisfied split,

to unite the day and
untie tomorrow,

to let joys joy,
to tether for yourself

togetherness.

Birthday Wish

The dog doesn't know he's a dog
though he knows all he needs
to know to be a dog.
That tree over there, the one
with two branches conducting
green music, can't spell
chlorophyll, or chill.
It does not bark like a dog.
The tree knows to shed its coat
when autumn comes, and
the dog senses he sheds
his fur in spring,
such contrary seasons
unconscious of being seasons
or seasons passing, just as
the dog won't know when
he's not a dog, and
the maple won't comprehend
the hatchet coming,
or the rot, or fire.
May I, like the dog, the tree,
their limbs, their bark,
their barklessness,
the coming fall, the fire,
the hatchet, and the rot,
know only what I need to be.

An Avocado for My Mother

You who in your petulant last years
loved only the richest fats and sweets,
didn't "care for" vegetables, declared
"There's a reason they call chicken fowl,"
ate bacon in belligerent portions,
kept your cheap stash of chocolates close
(secreted in your crossword drawer),

you with sons gone, God a question, bereft
of selves you made, now a lady left to pleasure,
your new habits a sharpened fork,
a trophy you had lived to deserve
like the stick of butter you stole and ate as a girl,

might enjoy the weighty berry of this avocado,
a fruit that of course you spurned in life,
if I can get you past its lizard skin to see
how it feels to me like the woman you were,
the way its rugged ovoid opens
to a firm tenderness, its determined seed
almost mahogany, a finial from
your grandmother's long-sold grandfather clock,
resistant like you to insults but
soon to gray and soften in the air,

so let me cup its cut vessel in my hand
and spoon the flesh and
lift it to your lips,
                    for here you are again,
a vibrant fifty in a violet summer dress,
risen to this occasion, reluctant but intrigued,

as you stick out your tongue
to test the texture, to see
if its savor is both buttery and sweet,
and swallow, for me,
                    as I eat my half,
happy enough that I got you to taste it.

A Boy's Own Heaven
    a friend asks me to pray for the soul of his dead brother

For you I go back to my boyhood dead,
said by my dad to hover above us
out of body but aflight in time,
pendant, weightless and waiting
like bees that shiver against the nectar, until
God raises their corpses to see their souls.
Such a tensed suspension for a boy to hold.
Dad didn't talk heaven much, as if
it was a prison we shouldn't visit,
as if suggesting it would bring it on
like the black cat crossing
or graveyard whistling,
like cloudbursts or raw luck,
like coins disappearing in a drain—
the cheery not-right-now right place
belied by the crying widow,

by you my friend whose brother now
in my grown life is terribly gone,
you who expect a resurrection that
for me in my avoidant ignorance is
now or never or then,
the dead bro dead or sleeping
or looking down on us in joy, or in
the waiting room with a tattered *Time*,
to be roused awake for judgment,
he who needs a prayer
like a dollar dropped on the street

or else is compost.
I cannot choose to choose.
I asked and ask what prayer, what help
we two could give to a God who,
if he is, does what he deigns, it seems,
without our asks, who grabs the wheel
and blows through every intersection. But

for you, my brotherless friend, you

who have a God who lives in a lattice
of a greater web you think we
humans can tug to make it
glisten like an angel's feather and
summon a net you think we quiver into,
your brother's salvation-filigree, I pray

to a dad and dud of a God
who may be diagnosably indifferent.
No matter my own dad whose form
has split from its cell of soul,
if soul is the word, but
like you says pray:
God of possible gossamer,
please let all of us brothers
entangle ourselves in embrace.

His Craft

For $50 my father bought
a tiny green boat, some eight feet
long, seafoam, color of a lily pad,
squared off at the bow, snub at the stern,
unmade to slice into water, built for no speed,
a craft sturdy on the stream, a donkey of a vessel
but willing, and with a curved, nearly flat bottom
where he could spread out his tackle and have lunch,
a boat to sit and float in, a boat that could take his bulk,
where from his seat he could cast and cast, cast and reel in
sunnies and perch he dreamed all winter, or not catch them,
be by himself or with maybe a single son bored in the bow.
If his body was a vessel it was this boat, near-solitary, with
its stalk of motor, resistant to its own oars but with mulish
momentum, sliding across tidewater, at home where salt
met fresh – the brack – fit for a man of mixed currents,
a man almost potable but bitter, tidal, rife with weeds,
ebb and rise, and anchored. Here he is near the reeds,
his arms tanned, hair misty in the sun, still wearing
his suspenders, his shirt white as an angel's chest,
casting, casting, not caring what the worm attracts,
beyond hunger, at home in the fishless afternoon
of what his father would call a day in the open,
his wife reading on the far shore in the shade,
his sons in sight on the dock, forever a
man in a cove at the edge of the bay,
sheltered, the river Styx a home,
the boat his harbor.

Days of 1996

I loved and slept with men
whose KS receded
in haphazard magic,
a time lapse in reverse,
all their awful acronyms
reinstated in the alphabet,
ghosts who got their bodies back.

I loved and slept with men
who didn't make the gate,
their HAART become ironic,
their states too opportunistic,
gone too far to be recalled.
In my dreams their gazes glisten,
the eyes of dogs at a kill shelter.

I love and sleep with a man
who is my lucky number,
my fluke, my Job's survivor.
And when I enter him,
in his body I find
and in my body he finds
the host of those we lost,
the congress of young men,
their faces faded and vivid,
their hands out.

After a Time I Touch My Husband

I don't mean to stroke him but I find I do,
the gesture of comfort abruptly rogue.
I run my hand down his pec, that warm stone,
take in the tang of his long day's skin.
A craving kindles in me, unwilling tinder,
a whiff of our first day, or maybe our second,
before we cut our paths inside each other,
as if a shudder of lightning strikes
in a junkyard, and in the years' debris
ignition flickers and fire flares,
fire become that tired desire that flames
up to the crotches of trees and sears them,
and wind arrives and disperses the sparks
into civilization, strewing them on our roof.

Turn

The box elder bugs are mating
on the sunny stucco wall,
their usual, urgent orgy,
butt to butt in an awkward
sex-spiral of a dance.
They stain if I squash them.
Even with crimson underwings
they are mostly unlike
choir members in lined robes,
though to imagine them singing
praise in their vertical church
is a nice erotic subversion.

When they frig and fly
I almost desire to be them,
two that spin as one,
to be that headlong,
a pas de deux aloft.
But still, all that libido,
all that balancing
on cement, wind current—
I am happier to be here,
content to stare,
a tall, human, stooping
voyeur whose white hair
makes him a dusty thistle
no insect would hit on.

They have no shame.
I think of myself and him
visible through the limbs
in that part of the park
when we were seen
and wanted to be, though
he reclasped his pants
and left for good.

Rain edges in,
drops populate

the box elder bugs' sky.
Maybe I hear thunder
or is it my tinnitus,
either way a different choir.

How weird not to want
fusion,
butt to butt or otherwise,
but instead elect to stay
fully clothed, unseen,
a single upright person,
feet on the ground,
my heart beating, not aching,
my head in the clouds.

Where Is the Lady

Where is the lady I was
when I was four,
a stole of blanket
around my neck,
a purse of a pail
exquisite on my wrist,
my heels held high,
toes sallied forward
on stilettos of air,
I the loveliest
mother's lovely friend,

caught up in my designs,
so dizzy with my perfume
I had to swan my cloud
wherever it was I walked,
no matter it was who looked,
their distaste a hazy buzz,

almost undeterred, almost,
by my father's regular scowl
as he waved his flat palm down,
a flash of signal that said
to drop my feet to the floor
of malehood we shared,

I the child he wished
would shed the girl like a dress,
weight the pail with sand,
run with the lift of Keds,
and keep an eye on the ball,
the being my mother assured
my father was a phase
for this Dr Spock of a kid,

but also the puzzling son
whose picture my father took,
developed, and showed,

whose photos are why I see
the vision of who I was,
the runaway fairy of child
when ladyship swelled in me
like a bodice or a bloodstream

until the purse no longer appealed,
or the heels hurt too much to bear
or children began their games
and shame was the weightiest mink,

and I shrugged on the boy
incited to put aside
the childish things of girls,
boyishness his resort,
who tethered himself to men,
who loved not trucks but cars
not for their engines but
for the lushness of their lines,
for the sleekness in their speed,
who came to love his gun,

who drove away whoever
she was he might have been,
not knowing who I could be
then or could be now,
this man who daily wears

a suit that seems to fit his frame,
his loafers almost light,
who can almost locate the scent
of the girl he sent to her room,
dressing for her party,
craving an invitation.

Like a Simile

My dead mother sneaks up on me
when I don't know I need her.
If a tiny piece of masonry,
the finger of a gargoyle, falls
inside me and I feel its current,
she appears without asking,
a glint of her sure self,

her own person but mine too,
and my body steps ahead,
I see my shadow move,
as if she's roused me for school,
as if I now know what to say.

As if when I'm dying
she will un-evanesce at my bedside,
a trick of the brain's electric flicker.
Or like that trick.
I've heard that happens but
I've never been close enough to know.

I wonder if the trick is all of it
or if the charge of the nerves
shutting down is as real as it gets,
the parent appearing because she appears.

It seems as if she should be there
because she was there at the start,
the mother of the thing,
half of the instigation,
the spring of the river
that is its own river.

I distrust apparitions,
I consent to science in my ignorance
of it and of spirit,
I rely on a rationale for which I have
no taxonomy.
Unlike faith, I take it on faith.

There she is again.
Or there is her notion.
Is she someone you know?

Today she sends me off
stronger in my senses,
my integument resilient,
like it or not.

Tomorrow or in ten years,
I ask you,
will she be my docent out?
It's as if I see her beckon me
beyond my nerves,

as if calling me into the car
she drives,
her left arm out the window,
already tanned,
the beauty marks darkening,

and as she steps on the gas

as if we are late for vacation,
my back goes back
to stick to the vinyl seat,
both of us with eyes on the road
as if,
because she knows where we went,
she knows where I am going.

I Want to Be Alone

Of eight billion of us
only one watches this patch
of creek, sits at this parting
of trees and reeds,
in this space and second,
unable even to step into
the same creek once.
What a break to leave behind
those who couldn't make it
because they are distant or dead,
with their catcalls and canticles.
Even mentioning them
doesn't summon them,
thank God or no one.
I relish their absence
and its opposite,
the absence of absence;
I decline to companion,
I shirk every inert assertion
of pantheism or hugging:
the creek patch a creek patch,
not what I make of the creek patch,
its differently celled creatures
just what we are.
If I see a mustard seed
I see a mustard seed
and leave it unseeded,
I step away from all signs,
even about the beaver traps
and the crocodile crossing,
all the specifics of species,
I see no Jesus tubing the flume,
I strip myself down
to wade in its wateriness,
shedding lexicon—
see, I have run out of words
and I hear thunder.

Snow Melting

Here my mission starts,
not in that harsh quilt
but in my seepage,
my diffusive self,

running out of who I am
into numbed soil,
into the systems,
the stunned, stilled roots,

bulbs layered in their coats
awaiting awakening,
minerals admixing in clay,
myself insinuating,

stealthing right to your casket—
not as resistant as they say—
to wake your body with
the wet warmth of decay

and kiss you into
a new, fifth season,
telling the apple tree to curl
an arm of root around

your coffin's shoulder so
the fruit when I'm forgotten
bears my fluid crunch
of crystals broken open,

and holds in sun and shade
the taste of human meat,
the body that departs declaring

let me like you be snowmelt,
let us be the disappearing
into the disappearing.

Nights of 2027

These days we try to forget
how Clay's HIV, even this discreet,
insinuates him into swifter aging,
every bike ride and squat a stay
to pacify the inflammation.
While I, his husband, negative
in virus and attitude, grizzle.
In 2027 the acrobatics of sex
and walking require consideration.
Every risk is a rehearsal.

Say it's 9/14/27, say it's Christmas.
It's a day we remember before it happens,
the day when one or both of us goes,
or our doctor, or a brother or sister,
or the corporate kid banker down the hall.
Say Cavafy's hankie salesman *poofs*
or his barista goes for good.
(Parents—they regressed past risk,
ghosts and stories gone for days.)

We won't exactly expect
the exits abrupt or extended:
the truant scooter, the diagnosis,
Clay's ember of infection a giant flame,
a plague, the plaque
detaching from my aorta wall,
the aorta itself dissecting.
But there we go.

Say the barbarians come at last.
We barely believe the globe
will give itself away,
strained too much in its traces
like a carriage horse on the street.
We half-expect an asteroid to land
on us latter-day dinosaurs in 2049
or else incineration in another year

whose rune or ruin you will know
if you're around to read a poem.

In the nights of 2027,
holding hands in bed,
entangled in our embrace,
we feel our heat in the blanket.
(Or maybe it's the night we cool.)
In the morning we lift the shade.
There's light and there's lack.

Suspense

Building this bridge they died,
venturing into the pilings,
then rising inside caissons
too fast. Their lungs exploded.
Through dying they taught
their survivors the science
of pressure, how humans
might measure, defy,
and heighten their depths.

From those gravestones hangs
the swaying weight of suspension,
the waver of roadway,
the roar of undulation that—
in a tension with vibration,
a flaw in the aeroelastics,
a flutter as in the atria
in some perfected resonance—
can send the structure down,

as will happen,
my car and I plunging
into seconds of suspense,
piercing New York Harbor,
pausing to consider
what it means to float,
then descending into
a building darkness,
then definite darkness,

becoming within,
the bay a human place,
my capsule of car and body
unsuspended and resting,
the rightful water seeping
and then sweeping in
before the divers arrive
to pluck me back to the sun,
my heart bursting.

A Friend Asks Me to Pray for the Soul of His Dead Brother

The flying cricket
in a frenzy of chirps
sketches my halo.

Maybe it harps on me
as the mate it aches for,
or else I hinder desire.

It blurs like a hand
making the sign of the cross
too fast and too long.

Finished, it spins off
into September cold,
a thread, an echo.

The World Without Me

The woodpecker eats in his Downeast tree—
frost edges in to kill the color.

West 22nd Street is cleaned. Cars repark.
The man from St. Francis Residence
walks thin, masked, and careful
down the sidewalk, his mind away.

The lake sways in slight wind and sunlight.

Someone remembers me nicely for an instant
and their phone trembles with a message.

The Hudson ebbs high on the pier—
something fishy, some tidal alteration.

A bird of some kind
scratches the mirror of lake—
some fish know to shirk her.

Someone reads my poem just to see
what she can steal for her poem.

Kids draw in chalk on another
street altogether, pleased at their distance.

A niece gives birth.

Someone wrestles in orgasm.
Someone else screams—
joy, pain, fear, I for one can't tell.

I was carried away in the flood,
ground between two stones.

By the lake or the river,
in a cove with freshly unstable sand,

or on the side of the mountain with
water receding from its roots,

a tree of some kind just falls down,
becoming driftwood, debris, or lumber.

Notes

Epigraphs: Emily Dickinson, *F775*; Oscar Wilde, *The Importance of Being Earnest*, third act.

"Photobomb, Taos, NM": The mountain in Taos, New Mexico, is known locally as Pueblo Peak. Some visitors call it Skull Mountain. Certain residents of the Taos Pueblo refer to it as Mó-ha-loh or Má-ha-lu. ("Land, Light and Legend of Taos: Taos Mountain sacred to all," by Larry Torres, *Taos News*, July 6, 2011.)

"I with No Rights in This Matter" takes its title from the penultimate line of "Elegy for Jane" by Theodore Roethke.

"A Boy's Own Bible Story" ("The father had business with his son…"): Genesis 22:1-16.

"A Boy's Own Bible Story" ("The weatherman is really mad…"): Genesis 5:32-9:28.

"A Boy's Own Bible Story" (*"You can make me clean…"*): Luke 5:12-16.

The "Days of" poems in this book are written after the "Days of" poems by Constantine P. Cavafy, Mark Doty, and James Merrill and employ some incidents and imagery related to those works. These poems also arise out of gratitude to Richard McCann's chapbook *Nights of 1990*, which in turn is a companion to Walt Whitman's "The Wound-Dresser."

"Days of 1996": HAART is an acronym for Highly Active Anti-Retroviral Therapy, the so-called "AIDS cocktail" regimens of drugs, introduced in 1995 and widely available at least in the United States in 1996, that can successfully suppress HIV and make infection with the virus a manageable condition in those people who have access to treatment.

Acknowledgements

Bennington Review: "Infinitive."

Best American Poetry Blog: "A Boy's Own Jesus."

The Cortland Review: "I with No Rights in This Matter" and "You're in My Light."

The Florida Review: "A Boy's Own Heaven" and "Days of 1985." Finalists for the 2022 *Florida Review* Poetry Award.

Great River Review: "Chaff" and "Photobomb, Taos," under the title "Photobomb Poem, Taos, NM."

HIV Here and Now: "Revival."

Humanities Review: "What Else."

New England Review: "Desert Stink Beetle."

On The Seawall: "My Mother" and "Malcah."

Poem-a-Day (Academy of American Poets): "Dead Deer."

Prairie Schooner: "Prodigal."

(Re) An Ideas Journal: "A Boy's Own Bible Story" (*"You can make me clean…"*), under the title "You Can Make Me Clean."

Reed: "A Boy's Own Bible Story" ("The father had business with the son…") under the title "Child Abuse."

Spoon River Poetry Review: "Disbelieving These Deaths, I Go to Sit by Lake Hebron." Winner of the 2020 Editors' Choice Award, selected by Austin Smith.

Still Against War: Poems for Marie Ponsot, 2016-2019 editions: "Grievance."

My thanks to all those who brought their care and insight to these poems, and all who helped bring them to readers, including Rick Barot, Sandra Beasley, Jan Beatty, Michael Broder, Jan Crawford, Maureen Daniels, Ruth Danon, Kwame Dawes, Sally Dawidoff, Alex Dimitrov, Mark Doty, Michael Dumanis, Jameson Fitzpatrick, Elisabeth Frost, Janlori Goldman, Christian Gullette, James Allen Hall, Kenneth Hart, Robert Hedin, Walter Holland, Amy Holman, Anna Maria Hong, Melissa Hotchkiss, Timothy Liu, Terry Lucas, Stephen Massimilla, Hermine Meinhard, Jerome Ellison Murphy, Felice Neals, Suzanne Parker, Marie Ponsot (1921-2019), Elaine Sexton, Soraya Shalforoosh, Sean Singer, Ron Slate, Austin Smith, Maggie Smith, Sarah van Arsdale, Brad Vogel, Michael Waters, Rob Weisbach, Baron Wormser, and Kirstin Hotelling Zona.

For the time and space to work on these poems, I am grateful to the Anderson Center for Interdisciplinary Studies, Jentel Arts, The Kimmel Harding Nelson Center for the Arts, the Helene Wurlitzer Foundation, Monson Arts, Poets Afloat, the Ragdale Foundation, the Ricci Road Residency, the Santa Fe Arts Institute, the Saltonstall Foundation, and the Virginia Center for the Creative Arts.

My thanks to Michelle Valladares and the faculty, staff, and students of the M.F.A. in Creative Writing Program at the City College of New York.

I am grateful for the support of my editors at Trio House Press: Kris Bigalk, Matt Mauch, and Tayve Neese.

My gratitude to my parents, the Reverend Addison Keiper Groff and Irene Bornemann Groff, and my brother, Jonathan Groff.

All love and thanks to Clay Williams.

About the Author

David Groff's previous book *Clay* was chosen by Michael Waters as winner of the Louise Bogan Award and published by Trio House Press. His first collection, *Theory of Devolution*, was selected by Mark Doty for the National Poetry Series. He completed *The Crisis of Desire: AIDS and the Fate of Gay Brotherhood* for its author, the Robin Hardy. With Philip Clark, he edited the anthology *Persistent Voices: Poetry by Writers Lost to AIDS*; with Jim Elledge, he edited *Who's Yer Daddy?: Gay Writers Celebrate Their Mentors and Forerunners*, which received a Lambda Literary Award. An independent editor book and publishing consultant, he teaches in the M.F.A. in Creative Writing Program of The City College of New York.

About the Artist

Michael Brohman is an artist and educator based in Denver, CO. He earned a Master of Architecture degree from the University of Colorado Denver and an undergraduate degree in Design and Ceramics from Colorado State University. He is on the faculty at the University of Colorado Denver as a Senior Instructor of Sculpture, and he has also taught sculpture in Scotland, Ireland, and China.

Michael has participated in artist residency programs at the Jentel Foundation and the Santa Fe Art Institute. His most recent exhibitions include solo shows at the University of Southern Mississippi Museum of Art in Hattiesburg, MS, the Whitney Center for the Arts in Sheridan, Wyoming and The Western Colorado Center for the Arts in Grand Junction, Colorado. Additionally, he has participated in three person shows at the Dairy Center for the Arts in Boulder and the Firehouse Art Center in Longmont, Colorado.

About the Book

Live in Suspense was designed at Trio House Press through the collaboration of:

Kris Bigalk and Natasha Kane, Editors
Joel W. Coggins, Cover Design
Michael Brohman, Cover Art
Hadley Hendrix, Interior Design

The text is set in Adobe Caslon Pro.

The publication of this book is made possible, whole or in part, by the generous support of the following individuals or agencies:

Anonymous

About the Press

Trio House Press is an independent literary press publishing three or more collections of poems annually. Our mission is to promote poetry as a literary art enhancing culture and the human experience. We offer two annual poetry awards: the Trio Award for First or Second Book for emerging poets and the Louise Bogan Award for Artistic Merit and Excellence for a book of poems contributing in an innovative and distinct way to poetry. We reserve the right to select other titles to publish from contest submissions.

Trio House Press adheres to and supports all ethical standards and guidelines outlined by the CLMP.

Trio House Press, Inc. is dedicated to the promotion of poetry as literary art, which enhances the human experience and its culture. We contribute in an innovative and distinct way to poetry by publishing emerging and established poets, providing educational materials, and fostering the artistic process of writing poetry. For further information, or to consider making a donation to Trio House Press, please visit us online at www.triohousepress.org.

Other Trio House Press books you might enjoy:

States of Arousal by Sunshine O'Donnell / 2022 Louise Bogan Award Winner, selected by Ed Bok Lee

The Fight by Jennifer Manthey / 2022 Trio Award Winner, selected by Aileen Cassinetto

Kaan and Her Sisters by Lena Khalaf Tuffaha / 2022

A Northern Spring by Matt Mauch / 2022

The Fallow by Megan Neville / 2021 Trio Award, selected by Steve Healey

Bloomer by Jessica Hincapie / 2021 Louise Bogan Award selected by Lee Ann Roripaugh

Unceded Land by Issam Zineh / 2021

Sweet Beast by Gabriella R. Tallmadge / 2020 Louise Bogan Award selected by Sandy Longhorn

The Traditional Feel of the Ballroom by Hannah Rebecca Gamble / 2020

Third Winter in Our Second Country by Andres Rojas / 2020

Songbox by Kirk Wilson / 2020 Trio Award Winner selected by Malena Mörling

YOU DO NOT HAVE TO BE GOOD by Madeleine Barnes / 2020

X-Rays and Other Landscapes by Kyle McCord / 2019

Threed, This Road Not Damascus by Tamara J. Madison / 2019

My Afmerica by Artress Bethany White / 2018 Trio Award Winner selected by Sun Yung Shin

Waiting for the Week to Burn by Michele Battiste / 2018 Louise Bogan Award Winner selected by Jeff Friedman

Cleave by Pamel Johnson Parker / 2018 Trio Award Winner selected by Jennifer Barber

Two Towns Over by Darren C. Demaree / 2018 Louise Bogan Award Winner selected by Campbell McGrath

Bird-Brain by Matt Mauch / 2017

Dark Tussock Moth by Mary Cisper / 2016 Trio Award Winner selected by Bhisham Bherwani

The Short Drive Home by Joe Osterhaus / 2016 Louise Bogan Award Winner selected by Chard DeNoird

Break the Habit by Tara Betts / 2016

Bone Music by Stephen Cramer / 2015 Louise Bogan Award Winner selected by Kimiko Hahn

Rigging a Chevy into a Time Machine and Other Ways to Escape a Plague by Carolyn Hembree / 2015 Trio Award Winner Selected by Neil Shepard

Magpies in the Valley of Oleanders by Kyle McCord / 2015

Your Immaculate Heart by Annmarie O'Connell / 2015

The Alchemy of My Mortal Form by Sandy Longhorn / 2014 Louise Bogan Award Winner selected by Peter Campion

What the Night Numbered by Bradford Tice / 2014 Trio Award Winner selected by Carol Frost

Flight of August by Lawrence Eby / 2013 Louise Bogan Award Winner selected by Joan Houlihan

The Consolations by John W. Evans / 2013 Trio Award Winner selected by Mihaela Moscaliuc

Fellow Odd Fellow by Stephen Riel / 2013

Clay by David Groff / 2012 Louise Bogan Award Winner selected by Michael Waters

Gold Passage by Iris Jamahl Dunkle / 2012 Trio Award Winner selected by Ross Gay

If You're Lucky Is a Theory of Mine by Matt Mauch / 2012

www.ingramcontent.com/pod-product-compliance
Lightning Source LLC
Chambersburg PA
CBHW022011120526
44592CB00034B/784